Confessions for Raising Winning Kids

by
Cathie Dorsch

(Of "Kids Like You")

Harrison House
Tulsa, Oklahoma

Unless otherwise noted, all Scripture quotations are taken from the *King James Version* of the Bible.

Scripture quotations marked AMP are taken from *The Amplified Bible. Old Testament* copyright © 1965, 1987 by Zondervan Corporation. *New Testament* copyright © 1954, 1958, 1987 by The Lockman Foundation. Used by permission.

2nd Printing
Over 20,000 in Print

Confessions for Raising Winning Kids
ISBN 0-89274-680-7
Copyright © 1996 by Cathie Dorsch
P. O. Box 22007
Little Rock, Arkansas 72221

Published by Harrison House
P. O. Box 35035
Tulsa, Oklahoma 74153

Dedication

To Abbie —

My Winner!

Acknowledgments

My special thanks to Pastor Happy and Jeanne Caldwell and to Agape Church, to my husband, John Dorsch, to my parents, Al and Ellen Prewitt, and to the Kids Like You Team, Jim and Cindy Grant, and John and Kaye Williams. Thank you for your love and support in reaching children.

Confessions for Raising Winning Kids

We all want kids who win. No parents *want* their children to fail and suffer in life, but few parents actually invest the kind of time it takes to make their children winners. On the other hand, our enemy spends plenty of "quality" time harassing our children. Today they face a host of challenges, problems, fears, and anxieties.

With this in mind, it is good to know that in spite of what may be happening in your family right now — through divorce, separation, financial, or family struggles — you can believe God for your children to come out on top.

Help Secure A Bright Future For Your Children

You can help your children avert disasters the enemy has "scheduled" for them. You can quench the devil's darts and confuse his plots.

You can prepare paths of safety, success, and health. And you can lay the groundwork for God to have His way in your children's lives — all by your confession. Then, as your children grow, you can teach them to confess the Word of God for themselves. When tests and trials come into their lives, they are prepared and equipped to gain the victory.

Begin to change your confession during your daily Bible reading. As you read the Scriptures each day, notice desires for your children quickening in your heart. You may be reading something in Psalms or Proverbs and it says exactly what you believe about a particular subject. That quickening, or heightened interest in a scripture, is the Holy Spirit giving you something He desires too — a scripture to confess over your children to start building that promise or truth into their lives.

The next step is to keep a prayer journal handy and mark these scriptures, adding them to your prayer and confession list. But the most important step comes next: Your confession over your children does not end in the prayer closet!

How you react to your children, what you call them, and how you respond to them all form your confession and go into their spirits as well. Suppose one of your children tells you at dinner (and I hope your family isn't eating around the television every night!) that he received a low test score that day. Do you react violently and scream, "Well, that's the last straw! You bonehead! You never could get that subject! What am I going to do with you? Didn't you study? Get out of here and don't tell me about another score like that until you've studied all night!"

Does that sound anything like you, or does the following scenario fit you better? In response to your child's announcement you calmly say, "Well now, let's talk about that. How did you study for the test? Do you need some help preparing for tests? You CAN get this material because you *can do all things through Christ who strengthens you.* Don't let

7

yourself think you can't get it. Let God help you. The anointing will be there to help you study and to take the test. You may have to give some extra time to studying, but you can pull up that grade."

Which reaction would you rather get as a child? Maybe your parents failed at supporting and helping you through crises. Don't make the same mistake with your children! As you confess God's Word over your children, let it be a two-edged sword and work on *you* as well. Let it correct your short-comings, and believe the Holy Spirit will guide you in your daily confessions over and conversations with your children.

Good Scriptures to Confess Over Your Children and Why

Let's look at some scriptures you can confess to lay a strong foundation in the lives of your children.

"You will keep them and preserve them, O Lord; You will guard and keep us from this [evil] generation for ever."
Psalm 12:7 (AMP)

If we read the newspapers or watch the news on TV often enough, we may begin to think it is better for our children never to leave the house! We are often afraid of certain schools, neighborhoods, and people because we are afraid of what *might* happen. This promise in Psalms should relieve our minds.

No matter where our children are, God is able to keep them from this evil generation. We can't control every classroom, family, or even estranged parent our children may visit or spend time with. However, if we are building this promise into their lives by frequent confession, we activate a force of protection around our children.

God Preserves, You Persevere

Some parents want to put all the pressure on God after confessing scriptures like Psalm 12:7. They say, "Oh well, I guess I will let my child spend the night with Bad Butch since he wants to, and God will just have to protect him." GUESS AGAIN!

You are the authority figure in the home and God honors authority. If you relinquish that authority by consciously making wrong decisions, you are asking for trouble. God will preserve your children, but you are a part of His hedge of protection. If you give them permission to be in evil situations without total peace from the Holy Spirit, you seriously compromise God's covering over your children.

Is the Holy Spirit giving you a "caution light" or "red flag" about an activity your children enjoy or certain people with whom they associate? That is God preserving your children by telling you when to say no. Learn to make those unpopular decisions when the Holy Spirit directs you to.

Although you may not always be able to give your children a concrete answer, you can say with confidence, "I think we'd better wait on that," or "I'm not comfortable with this. I think you need to find somebody else to go to the party with you." You cannot teach your children to be led by peace and then make decisions for them that do not give you peace!

> "The law of the Lord is perfect, restoring the [whole] person; the testimony of the Lord is sure, making wise the simple. The precepts of the Lord are right, rejoicing the heart; the commandment of the Lord is pure *and* bright, enlightening the eyes.... Moreover by them is your servant warned, [reminded, illuminated, and instructed]; and in keeping them there is great reward."
> Psalm 19:7-8,11 (AMP)

A very beautiful and well-known psalm, this passage can pave all kinds of clear paths for your children. If divorce has disrupted their personalities and sense of security, the Word of God can restore the whole person — spirit, soul, and body. If depression has plagued any of your children, the Word of God you confess can cause their hearts to rejoice. If they have struggled in their studies or in relationships, God's Word can make them wise and enlighten them. If they get into a compromising situation, a simple verse of

Scripture can remind them of God's will, instruct them in what to do, and even warn them of danger.

As you begin your confession and prayer time, remind God that these promises are His Word. As you call out each one of them, expect them to go into effect in the lives of your children — even when it looks like the opposite is happening! This passage is a good daily confession and will give the Holy Spirit a wide entrance into the hearts of your children.

Supernatural Protection and Provision

For the sake of space I will not print Psalm 91 in its entirety, but take a few minutes to read it before you read further.

Every verse is power-packed. Why should you fear drive-by shootings, attacks at school, kidnapping, or sexual abuse? You can see in this psalm that God desires to provide a realm of protection that is *supernatural*. We may lock our doors at night, leave our children with the best baby-sitters, and take lots of extra precautions, but there is no substitute for the supernatural intervention of angels and Holy Ghost protection over our children!

Our "Kids Like You" Team regularly assists in inner-city crusades. We are often saddened by what some of the children to whom we minister must face. Many of them sleep in their clothes for fear and necessity. They do not know if they may have to jump up and run for their lives in the night. That kind of fear, the kind you can "taste," should not have to be experienced by any child, but particularly the children of God.

As you read carefully through Psalm 91, confess that your children dwell in the secret place of the Most High; that surely God will deliver them from snares; that no evil shall befall them nor any plague or calamity come near them; that God's angels have a special charge to keep, defend, and preserve them in all their ways; that God will be with them in trouble, will deliver them, and will satisfy them with long life.

> **"Bless the Lord, O my soul: and all that is within me, bless his holy name. Bless the Lord, O my soul, and forget not all his benefits: Who forgiveth all thine iniquities; who healeth all thy diseases; Who redeemeth thy life from destruction; who crowneth thee with lovingkindness and tender mercies; Who satisfieth thy mouth with good *things; so that* thy youth is renewed like the eagle's."**
>
> **Psalm 103:1-5**

Here is our Comprehensive Health Care and Management Plan with full benefits — and what a package! Moms and dads want to provide so many things for their children, but sometimes they just can't do it all. *But God can!* He can supply their need of salvation, ongoing forgiveness, health, protection from harm, and all the other good things they need.

If you are a single parent, trust God to make up the difference for you. I have prayed with many single parents who face feelings of inadequacy. They fear they cannot provide what two parents could. God will make up the difference, however, as you confess these blessings. He will be the other parent for you. He will help you as a parent and will reveal His nature as a loving Father to your children *Himself*.

Psalm 103:1-5 contains some key points I want to look at individually:

1. *Bless the Lord*. Start and end your confessions by blessing the Lord. You don't have to nag God about your children — or whine about them! God works through His Word, so bless Him confidently, knowing your confessions are working in your children's lives. Instead of whining or nagging, rest in the Lord and give Him the voice of rejoicing.

2. *Forgiveness*. If God can forgive all of your children's sins, so can you. Don't bring up old mistakes when dealing with new ones. Let sins drop after the discipline and instruction period have passed. Deal with them in a

loving, forgiving attitude, not a hostile "I'm still mad at you" attitude. Start each day new, as God's mercies do, and give your children a happy, forgiven send-off into their day.

Confessing and releasing God's forgiveness over your children frees them of past sins and mistakes. It decreases the power of sin, minimizes its wages, and maintains unity in your home. Jesus told his disciples that those whose sins they forgave were forgiven. (See John 20:23.)

3. *Healing.* Why suffer through anguishing childhood diseases, missed school, poor health, and physical weakness in your children? The Word of God clearly promises that the stripes of Jesus paid the price for our healing. (See 1 Peter 2:24.) Attack sickness and don't let it rob your children of the abundant life God has planned for them. Confess, "Father, I bless and praise You that allergies have to get out of my children. In Jesus' Name, my children are not tormented through their childhood with disease. Their bodies are

16

strong and able in Your service, for You heal every one of our diseases." (See Psalm 103:3.)

4. *Redemption from Destruction*. Many children in our society face problems and situations that try to rob them of the peace and security they have in Jesus. They may live in a broken home or with an abusive parent. Some children I minister to bear the pain of such broken or abusive lifestyles.

If you and your children are coming out of such destruction, you will see God redeem the lives of your children as you confess Psalm 103:1-5. These verses can be very helpful to parents, but especially single parents, who suffer guilt over the harm their past decisions may have brought to their children. Any parent in any situation can put the past behind them and believe the promise of God to bring the sparkle back into their children's eyes.

5. *Satisfying Their Mouths With Good Things*. Childhood and adolescent years should be enjoyed, filled with many happy memories and successes. Sometimes parents face hard

times financially and are unable to provide all they want for their children.

As I shared earlier, God can provide what you cannot. As you pray this promise over your child, you are declaring that God is satisfying their mouth with good things, so that their youthfulness is renewed, not robbed through hard times and financial lack.

The pressures of job and family will come soon enough in adulthood, so believe God will satisfy your child with good things, giving him the desires of his heart. God's children should be the ones in school who are promoted and elevated into good positions, where they can be even brighter witnesses for Him. Childhood and teen years should be filled with many successes!

Furthermore, during tough times we should believe and confess God's Word, teaching our children by our example. Seeing God's Word in action in our lives shows our children that they can rely on God's promises. Then, as Psalm 103:5 promises, He will satisfy us with good things and give us the desires of our hearts.

> **"But my God shall supply all your need according to his riches in glory by Christ Jesus."**
>
> **Philippians 4:19**

There are times when you need to get out from under the pressure of having to provide everything and allow your children the opportunity to use their faith too. Then they will also say "my God supplied my need, not my mom and dad." By confessing this scripture over your children, you also can get a jump on those times when your children's needs exceed your budget — like when they need braces or a car.

The Word Brings Peace

> **"My son, keep thy father's commandment, and forsake not the law of thy mother.... When you go, it shall lead you, when you sleep, it shall keep you, and when you awake, it shall talk with you."**
>
> **Proverbs 6:20,22**

Confess that your children obey your instructions and God's Word, so they — and you — will live in peace. Rebellion and disobedience plague our society from every angle, but children who have been taught to obey God's Word bring rest and peace to their homes, classrooms, jobs, or wherever God may lead them.

As you confess God's Word over your child, it has an avenue to talk with them. The first words in their spirit each morning should be words from the Word of God. Proverbs 6:22 says the Word will lead your children wherever they go, talk with them throughout the day, and keep them when they sleep.

God's Word guards them not only in their waking hours, but also during the time in which they sleep. Young children spend almost half of their 24-hour day sleeping in order to keep up with their rapid physical, mental, and emotional development. Praying and confessing the Word of God over them as they sleep will give them sweet, peaceful rest.

And, if you've prayed and confessed the Word over them and with them during the day, bedtime will not be something your child will fear.

> **"And all thy children shall be taught of the Lord, and great shall be the peace of thy children."**
>
> **Isaiah 54:13**

Invite the Lord to teach your children, to talk with them through the day, as they put things together, and play with other children. Invite the Holy Spirit to be your children's teacher, and great peace will result. When God leads your children, talks with them, and teaches them, they can enjoy great peace. Let's look at some key points about this peace.

1. *It's Great.* By definition, "great" peace in Isaiah means abundant, exceeding, enough, mighty, manifold, frequent in its appearance, and sufficient to cover any situation. (See James Strong, *Exhaustive Concordance of the Bible* #7227.) Your children may face numerous trials, but God's peace is manifold in its nature and can cover each trial.

2. *Undisturbed Composure.* The Amplified Bible says, "great shall be the peace and undisturbed composure of your children." That kind of peace, the Hebrew word, "shalom," means to be in good health and have well being, safety, and security. (See James Strong, *Exhaustive Concordance of the Bible* #7965.)

Taught by the Best

When you think about it, the Lord's offer to be the Teacher of our children is wonderful. To be taught of Jesus is to become intimate with Him, discipled, and wise. He desires to disciple our children so they are accustomed to His voice and will readily obey Him.

No matter how much godly teaching and training we give our children, they have to know God for themselves. By developing the habit of spending regular time with God, they become God's students and pave the way for a bright future!

"I can do all things through Christ which strengtheneth me."

Philippians 4:13

Literally translated, Christ means "The Anointed One." (See James Strong, *Exhaustive Concordance of the Bible* #5547.) The anointing is there to strengthen them to do right over wrong no matter what the circumstances. Build into your confessions and your conversations with your children lots of "I cans" and eliminate the "I can'ts."

My father was a great motivator for me when I was growing up. He did not put up with whiny little Cathie crying, "I can't do this!" He *always* responded with an old country expression, "Can't never did do nothin'!" It wasn't good English, but I sure got the point. I could envision an old guy named "Can't" who couldn't do anything, and I didn't want to be like him! Dad's words would always give me the strength to try again.

How much more is the anointing of God available to help your children "try again." Nurture your children's talents. Be an encourager. Let the anointing be your children's encourager as well. God saw the

23

future of Jacob and Esau when he told their pregnant mother, Rebecca, "two nations are in thy womb" (Genesis 25:23). Help your children see their future and their possibilities if they lean on the Lord Jesus Christ and on the power of the Holy Spirit.

Get A Life With God!

"Daniel purposed in his heart that he would not defile himself.... As for these four children, God gave them knowledge and skill in all learning and wisdom: and Daniel had understanding in all visions and dreams.... And in all matters of wisdom and understanding, that the king inquired of them, he found them ten times better than all the magicians and astrologers that were in all his realm."

Daniel 1:8,17,20

How appropriate for today's kids! Your children must have their own living, breathing relationship with Almighty God — not just experience Him through you. Encourage this at all times and at all ages of your children. Confess that they know and walk with God, making a stand for Him like Daniel and the Hebrew children.

Daniel's relationship with God was the secret to his success. It brought him spiritual understanding, mental alertness, social favor, and material rewards. As you confess the above scriptures, you are assaulting mental deficiencies, learning disabilities, short-comings, and mental blocks. Through their relationship with God, you are helping your children actually become *more intelligent*.

These verses in Daniel, chapter 1, speak separately of wisdom and understanding as qualities granted to Daniel even above "skill in learning." Your children can possess these same qualities. When they encounter a society that is hungrily seeking "the unseen world" through New Age philosophies, psychics, or other ungodly avenues, they can be beacons of God's light to their peers and be found "ten times better."

Conclusion

As you begin to pray God's Word, you will see the Holy Spirit add to your skill in parenting. You will sense more of the leading and guidance of the Holy Spirit in your dealings with your children. You will know things about them only He could tell you. God will give you sneak previews of your children's futures and you will sense His call on your children's lives.

Confess God's Word daily and believe you will be more sensitive to the gifts of the Holy Spirit operating in your home. You need them, your spouse needs them, and your children need them. *The gifts of the Spirit are not just for church; they are for you and your home.*

Finally, you will grow in the anointing — the anointing to reach your children, to communicate with them, to handle and love them, to pray for their success, and to pray powerfully. Mary and Joseph could have had overwhelming feelings of inadequacy to raise

God's Son, Jesus, but God gave them an anointing that was sufficient to meet the challenge.

Mary and Joseph received the grace of God for their task, and He will do no less for you. Like Jesus, your children have a race to finish and a call to fulfill. And like Mary and Joseph, God has an anointing for you to parent your children. Through the Anointed One, receive it and walk in it!

Confessions for Winning Kids
(Based on Indicated Scripture)

My children can do all things through Christ Who strengthens them.

Philippians 4:13

My God supplies all my children's needs according to His riches in glory by Christ Jesus. They see God move for them and on their behalf, and know God for themselves as Provider and Father.

Philippians 4:19, Genesis 21:17

Greater is He who is in my children than he that is in the world.

I John 4:4

God has not given my children a spirit of fear, but of power, of love, and of a sound mind.

2 Timothy 1:7

My children have great peace, for they are taught of the Lord. God is teaching and talking with my children today.

Isaiah 54:13

God is preserving them from this evil generation forever...preserving them wherever they may go, preserving them from bad relationships, and preserving them from danger.

Psalm 12:7

My children hearken unto me and to God's Word and dwell safely, quiet from the fear of evil.

Proverbs 1:33

No weapon that is formed against them shall prosper. They are far from oppression. There shall no evil befall them nor any plague come near their dwelling, for God has given his angels special charge over them to keep, defend, and preserve them all the days of their lives.

Isaiah 54:14,17; Psalm 91:10,11

My children can lay down in peace and sleep, for you, O Lord, will have them only to dwell in safety.

Psalm 4:8

They obey God's Word and mine, and the Word keeps them when they sleep, talks with them when they awaken, and guides them in the way they should go.

Proverbs 6:20-23

I correct my children and they give me rest. My children honor their parents, are obedient and well-pleasing to the Lord. It is well with my children all the days of their lives, and God satisfies them with a long, peaceful, and happy life.

Proverbs 29:17; Colossians 3:20;
Ephesians 6:2,3

My children have the mind of Christ, an anointed mind. They are quick to learn and have success in school. They are renewed in the spirit of their minds. Like Daniel, they stand for God and God blesses them with skill in learning, in wisdom and in understanding. In all matters they are found to be ten times better than the devil's children.

1 Corinthians 2:16; Daniel 1:8-21;
Ephesians 4:23

I bless the Lord with all that is within me and bless His Holy Name, for He loads my children with benefits. I release today's benefits to my children. I will not forget one of His benefits and declare them to be in operation in my children's lives. Bless

You, Lord, for you forgive all my children's iniquities, and I forgive them, releasing the power of forgiveness in their lives.

Bless the Lord, for You are healing every one of their diseases. Health and strength flow in their bodies, and the diseases of this earth and generation cannot prosper in them.

Bless You Lord, for You are redeeming their lives from destruction, crowning them with tender mercies and acts of loving kindness, and You are satisfying their mouths with good things so that their youth is renewed like the eagle's. Their strength is made overcoming and soaring. They are satisfied by God and they do not hunger after what the world and sin have to offer.

Psalm 103:1-6; Psalm 68:19

The Word of God that I am declaring over my children will not return void. Its power and nature is producing life in my children. It is rejoicing their hearts, restoring their whole person, enlightening their eyes, and making them wise; moreover, by it my children are warned, and in keeping it, they experience great reward.

Isaiah 55:11; Psalm 19:7-11

My children give no place to the devil today. They overcome by the blood of the Lamb and the Word of His testimony. They are strong in the Lord and in the power of His might. They are covered in the whole armor of God, and the shield of faith quenches all the fiery darts of the wicked one. They resist the devil who flees from them this day.

My family is walking in the fruit of the spirit, and I will follow the quickening of the Holy Spirit. Together and as individual believers, we will not grieve the Holy Spirit. We will not let the sun go down on our wrath. The gifts of the Holy Spirit are in operation in my family. I thank you, Father God, for the anointing to raise my children to fulfill Your plan, Your will, and Your purpose, in Jesus' Name.

Ephesians 4:26-30; Revelation 12:11;
Ephesians 6:10,16; James 4:7;
Galatians 5:16,22; 1 Corinthians 12:7

Teach Your Winners To Confess These Truths:

I am a child of God — Romans 8:16.

I am redeemed from the curse of the law — Galatians 3:13.

I am blessed coming in and going out — Deuteronomy 28:6.

I am a new creature in Christ Jesus — 2 Corinthians 5:17.

I am led by the Spirit of God — Romans 8:14.

I am kept in safety wherever I go — Psalm 91:11.

I am strong in the Lord and in the power of His might — Ephesians 6:10.

I am healed by the stripes of Jesus — 1 Peter 2:24.

I am more than a conqueror through Him who loves me — Romans 8:37.

I am renewed in the spirit of my mind — Ephesians 4:23.

I am the light of the world and the salt of the earth — Matthew 5:13,14.

I am an imitator of God as a dear child — Ephesians 5:1.

I obey my parents and am well pleasing to the Lord — Colossians 3:20.

I honor my father and mother, it is well with me all the days of my life, and I live a long life — Ephesians 6:1-3.

I cast all my cares on Jesus for He cares for me — 1 Peter 5:7.

I can do all things through Christ who strengthens me — Philippians 4:13.

I have favor with God and man — Proverbs 3:4.

I have authority over all the power of the enemy, and nothing shall by any means hurt me — Luke 10:19.

I have the mind of Christ — 1 Corinthians 2:16.

I overcome by the blood of the Lamb and the word of my testimony — Revelation 12:11.

I sleep in peace for God would have me to only dwell in safety — Psalm 4:8.

I hear the voice of the Good Shepherd, and the voice of a stranger I will not follow — John 10:4,5,14.

Great is my peace for I am taught of the Lord — Isaiah 54:13.

No weapon formed against me shall prosper — Isaiah 54:17.

Greater is He that is in me than he that is in the world — 1 John 4:4.

God has not given me a spirit of fear, but of power, love, and a sound mind — 2 Timothy 1:7.

My God shall supply all my need according to His riches in glory by Christ Jesus — Philippians 4:19.

About the Author

Cathie Dorsch is an associate minister at Agape Church in Little Rock, Arkansas, under Pastor Happy Caldwell, where she has served since 1980. She helped to pioneer and lead its children's ministry, and also founded its children's television outreach, "Kids Like You." This dynamic program began on Little Rock's NBC affiliate in 1984 and quickly grew in popularity. It is now airing nationally and internationally with numerous broadcasting awards to its credit.

Cathie's background in children's theater has helped her to create lively characters and memorable ways of reaching children. With the Kids Like You Team, she helps establish children's ministries in other nations and frequently speaks on effective children's ministry. Cathie and the Team also conduct rallies in schools, camps, conferences, and churches.

Along with her ministerial role at Agape Church, Cathie teaches in the Agape School of

World Evangelism and is active in inner-city outreach. She is married to John Dorsch and has one daughter, Abbie.

To contact Cathie and Kids Like You, you may write or call:

Cathie Dorsch
Kids Like You
P. O. Box 22007
Little Rock, Arkansas 72221
1-800-264-2525

Other books by Harrison House are
available at your local
Christian bookstore.

Harrision House
Tulsa, Oklahoma

Harrison House Vision

Proclaiming the truth and power
Of the Gospel of Jesus Christ
With excellence;

Challenging Christians to
Live victoriously,
Grow spiritually,
Know God intimately.